Collected Poems 1
1985-1999

Jamie Inglis

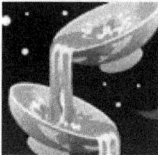

© PROHIBITED PUBLICATIONS
MMXX

collected poems 1 1985-1999
© Jamie Inglis 2020. All rights reserved.
First Edition 2009
Paperback Second Edition 2020
ISBN 978-1-9163542-0-3

Many thanks to Jim Dalziel for kind permission to reproduce
'*Amazed Man*', '*Boffin*', '*Beached Writer*', '*Breton Band*',
the '*Milestone Icon*', '*Pleased to meet you Mr Lear*',
'*Isosceles*' and '*Serious Birthday Card*'.
Many thanks to Alex Nisbet for kind permission to reproduce
'*Spring*', '*Geisha*' and '*Karaoke Kabuki*'.

Black hole passing a star and Hubble telescope images © NASA/JPL.
All photographs and other images © Jamie Inglis 2020.

New Neologisms - new words for new times www.newneologisms.com
The Disorganised Society - real life is disorganised   www.disorganised.org
Burning the Page - from Paper to Pixel   www.burningthepage.com
The Science Fiction Index - The best of all time   www.sci-fi-index.com
We publish everything, we publish everywhere www.prohibitedpublications.com

Created with Lulu

Published by
PROHIBITED PUBLICATIONS
79 Bruntsfield Place
Edinburgh
EHIO 4HG
Scotland

ISBN 978-1-9163542-0-3

9 781916 354203 >

also by jamie inglis

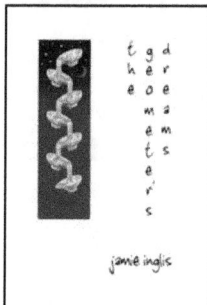

the geometer's dreams
(1992)

fractals & mnemonics
(1996)

hold on
(2000)

gluon notes
(2006)

experience engines
(2010)

Discovered Roads
(2018)

Warning

Do **not** look inside
Do **not** turn this page
Do **not** go any further

Do **not** stop now
Do **not** look up
Do **not** listen further

Do **not** speak
Do **not** ask
Do **not** question

Do **not** see
Do **not** imagine
Do **not** understand

Do **not** think
Do **not** wonder
Do **not** refuse

Do **not** turn
Do **not** worry
Do **not** change

Do **not** stand
Do **not act**
Do **not** move

Do **not** look
Do **not** listen

Do **not** do this
Do **not** do that
Do **not** now stop

Do **not** do
Do **not**hing

Do **not** do anything
Do **not** do now
Do **not** do nothing

Contents

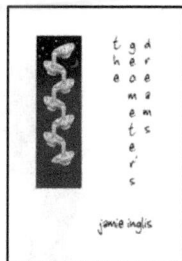

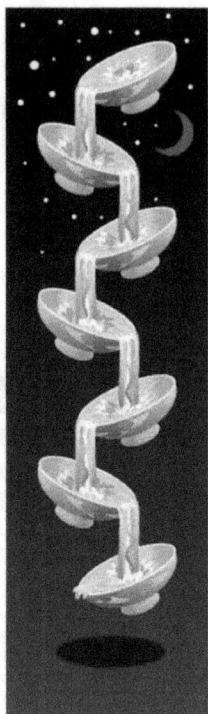

the geometer's dreams

jamie inglis

the geometer's dreams

Jamie Inglis

Contents - *'the geometer's dreams'*

in general

Cont.

Cont.

from a frontline living room

of the Gulf War

on the move

on postcard landscapes

Cont.

Cont.

on postcard landscapes cont.

from a possible future

at last

in general

Standing at the feet of giants,
Belem, Portugal © Alison Boyd

CHINESE   AND   THE
BOX   THE   GEOMETER

prying   from   for   Looking

eyes.   all   Secrets.   at

but   Hidden   life

First contact, train to Edinburgh

The fragile nectar of first contact
with hastily averted eyes
or inadvertent touch.

An exploration of potential meaning
in that moment of meeting
of two strangers, unknown till now.

But now that moment has altered
and lack of strangeness

beckons.
An intermingling of lines
perhaps love, perhaps passion
perhaps hate, perhaps danger.

Continuation as an instant decision
in a moment
of subliminal processes
hidden from interception by a conscious
Touch.

A simple spillage at Camelford

6th July 1988,
Unattended Lowermore Waterworks,
Camelford, North Cornwall.

Twenty Tons of Aluminium Sulphate
are dumped in the water supply.
Thirty thousand tons of dilute / Pollute the future.
A strong acid pH of 2.8 assists the toxin
dissolving copper and lead from pipes in passing.

The first glass.
Dizzy, stomach cramps.
The tea looks terrible, full of sludge and watery.
Sickness and diarrhoea begins.
Hair dyed green then skin rashes and mouth ulcers appear.
This is how it starts.

The pharmacist is emptied of patent remedies
for the mouth ulcers and diarrhoea.
The GP's morning surgery is busy today.

At Lowermore the Aluminium level is noticed to be low.
Where is the missing supply?
Now the wrong delivery is noticed.
Three hundred thousand tons flushed out in error
killing the river.
Dead fish float ten feet below the weir
and news arrives of the lambs that died.

Doctor Newman discovers 70% of the population affected.
The Water Authority reassures.

Cont.

Cont.

Dame Barbara Clayton's committee
attributes the effects to anxiety.

Probable long term effects include -
Arthritis and Alzheimer's.
Short exposures to high levels gives -
      deposits in bone
      and throughout the body
      including the brain.
Conducted by transferrin
across that all important final blood brain barrier.
Even the visitors take the toxin home.

Then news of club feet in excess
in in-utero children exposed, who,
poisoned, lay still in the womb

Later the dementia begins
in the right hemisphere,
        disturbing
    visual-spacial abilities.

Later still.
Speech
ends

The skyscrapers tears

The skyscrapers cry
large brown tears
from many single windows
covering the walls
with spreading stains.

The heights of the city
looking out
surveying the sites
from lonely skies
with damp eyes.

Standing in silence
weeping in the rain
a heart above the city
showing its pain,
coalescing, as tears.

Both

Necrosis and Nectar
defining the length
of individual days.
The discreteness of moments
as capsules of experience
shuffled in short-term
memories reviewing loop.
Some for disposal
some for saving.
The pain and the pleasure
making the day.

What next

Moving to the moon.
The notion surely,
of a loon.
Besides methinks,
it's much too soon.

Mondays Poems

Collecting poems on Mondays
the atheists day of rest.
From a previous week of work
with pen and eye and ear.

Collecting poems
of imagination at work.
Littered through the week
as complete, untitled, unfinished.

Poems on Mondays
as catharsis of play.
Scattered winds of the week
as ideas, rhymes and fun.

Collecting poems on Mondays
the enjoyment of the week.
Purely for fun
leaving the *detritus de trop.*

The worst has happened

What could you possibly choose
as the worst thing, ever invented?

Perhaps you would laugh first,
thinking of the bane of your life.
Maybe the car, the television
or something too ridiculous for words.
Like a big mac or a deep pan pizza.

Some people are bound to be serious,
talking of atom bombs and gas chambers.
But do these things actually count
if they have so little effect on your life
but a sense of outrage.

The worst thing ever invented
must make you laugh.
Only something funny and bad
could possibly be a contender for worst.
Only when we reach the nadir do we laugh.
When it can't get any worse.
That's when it's got to be funny.
That recognition that the worst
has *already* happened.

This island

This island earth
drowning in its own sea
of population.

As they struggle for breath
from a decaying atmosphere
of accelerating poison.

Stomaching silent starvation
in growing masses
moving from barren fields.

Their migration hastened
by affluence and waste
in distant lands.

Turning fields into deserts
waiting for the flooding
of the rest of this island.

On the beach

Every couple a different distance
Apart in their apparent union
Alone, as only lovers can be
In secret hidden solitude
Of routine unseen manners

And painful sores subconsciously avoided
As the joy begins to fade
With each ageing anniversary
What remains between each two
Is always a different distance

Thought of mortality

Every thought anew
a marker of mortality
acquired in life's footsteps,
as the history unwinds.

What treadmarks of fate
continue to wait
each ready to print
the next unseen mark.

The XXIVth Annual Seminar on Infection

A concerto of information from speakers
delivered in womb-like student darkness.
Energetic academia blinking and sliding
the performance providing reminding clues.
Ease of digestion the bones of infection
course of containment necessary to prevention.

A holiday school in disaster management
considering the failures of previous experts.
Learning natures lessons by retrospective analysis
of medical knights supplying appropriate timbre.
Weight of control in rule application
as communicable disease everywhere abounds.

What makes the difference is society's progress
provision of mass and ease of convenience.
Centralised eating at junk food troughs
creating the problems for public health.
Now the trend is organic and conscientious
new problems appearing, no end in sight.

Burger is King

Swimming amidst mass-produced food.
Consumer non-durable and not
guaranteed to do you a lot of good.
No taste, No flavour, No wonder.

We lack interest and it shows
in the junk food we shovel.
For this is the absolute nadir
of late twentieth century cuisine.
Food as fast calories and profit,
an exact formula, excluding
        health
        taste
        variety
        etc.

i'm not loving it campaign

Do you see this nothing

A name/title on the door/lapel
removes the personality inside
from having to extend/express
within/beyond these confines.

Who are you now?
Lost behind this name
as a plate/badge for
you/the world to know/see.

Do you see this nothing
that has become of you.
As the door closes behind
the world stops for

For William Styron
'Darkness Visible'

Touched by the cloak of madness
bringing the depths of darkness
and the isolation of depression
removing every contact impression.

Shutting down the active life
as dysfunction and inner strife
generate a solitary alienness
enclosing the mind with stress.

Of surviving each heavy day
of melancholy day after day.
And losing continuing will
no hope no desire still.
Lost from a saving emotion
by the weight of dark in motion.

Creature of thought

In a garden very far away
an empty wooden bench seat waits.
The bench of parks and every council.
Welcoming and familiar
with simple humble donation plaque -

```
For Mrs Irene Wilson
A keen gardener
```

An inviting seat for all
to rest in a secluded corner.
Pulling the view in close
to be part of the gardens stillness.
The sound and blossom smell
of peace and ease resting here.

A contemplation spot above all others
in a haven of memories escape.
This alcove of nature's tranquillity
where the creatures of thought repose.

Virus Latin Poison

Magic simplest smallest form of life
replicating chemical from the dawn of time.
An inert agent waiting for life outside
becoming hidden, part of an unsuspecting host.

Only one success at eradication so far
as the world is vaccinated to wipe out a species.

We have no preferred place in nature
as competitors wait in hidden sites.
First samples from Africa, the naming continues
Marburg, Nile, Ebola, Rift Valley,
An unknown source, an unseen reservoir,
places on the map as point sources.
An emerging litany of competition.

A steady rate of mutation in the swarm
then $R_0 > 1$ produces the disease epidemic.
HIV is winning the battle so far.
Will the next be the last for man.

Hope in our time

The Hope syndrome
Genetic part of every psyche

The Hope complex
A belief made purpose

The Hope phenomenon
The credo of our time

The Hope cartel
Sold to us a panacea

The Hope agenda
For only a limited few

The Hope debate
Our future lowered to discussion

The Hope dilemma
The choices of Solomon

The Hope gallery
An exhibition of dreams

The Hope market
The province of aspirations

Before the storm

Before the storm,
quality sharply alters.

Before the storm,
the sunlight quality sharply alters.
Dispersing the fogginess of summer days haze,
lifting veils as daylight falters.
Outlines sharpened from visions maze.

Before the storm,
the air quality sharply alters.
Dispersing the heaviness of summer days.
Lifting clear of turgid quality,
fresh, intoxicating, from perfumes prison.

Before the storm,
the sound quality sharply alters.
Dispersing the chorus of summer's days.
Lifting hearing from restless voices,
a stillness unique in auditory repertoire.

Before the storm,
a moment of discernible quality.
Cleanly sweeping the daze away,
as nature's hand lifts and changes.
Bringing the rain.

Boatwatching

White crescents line abreast on the shore
Sleeping nights at rest from the race
Perched pensively, yet clearly out of place
Silent and still, the waterline a pace
Beached skeletal crucibles on ungainly solid floor

The early light brings breaths of wind
And eager weekend sailors in search of water
Assembling masts and sails ready for later
Preparing the crew and pulling on gaiters
Talking tactics and preparing to contend

Practice over now waiting for the gun
Then off in a flurry of red triangles
Cutting through water a contrast of angles
Tacking and turning to worry about less
Thrills and enjoyment simply for fun

Strings of shapes strung in mobile lines
Circles of keels and occasional toppling
The jibs and spinnakers flowing and airing
Each graceful move adjusted and sparing
Every sharp reflection on the water shines

Interlocking wakes disrupting the surface
Cruising in patterns not far from shore
The intricate glides searching for more
Knots to come home at least seconds before
To clip the line, winning the race

Into the exhibition

Pushing through the doors to the exhibition
turning aside for a moment
from the routine pavements
and intent Saturday afternoon shoppers
collecting their weekly purchases of life
flowing outside too focused to see
enclosed and encased in numberless sub-routines.

Releasing the clacking door on the outside
left inside on an unknown land / world
full of many different dreams
by unknown names in unexpected hues.

Looking round and getting a different
view of many unexpected lives
revealed on canvas or
by implication in the observation.

Finding a mixture of pleasure
and ?/ incomprehension
shuffling round the distorted (circular) square
smiling and scowling at the presented visions
till all the vistas have passed
leaving nothing purchased for life
but new routes
pushing through the doors out of the exhibition.

Remembering the Eighties

How shall we remember the eighties
the penultimate decade of the last millennium?
Will our view be affected by perspective
or the change that has occurred within us.

We shall remember the changes in our lives
both looked for, struck and simply arrived.
And those near and far at the start
how they've closed, parted, lived and changed.

But what shall we remember of the rest
but an impression of newspaper and television.
How it affected and changed our self-view
with respect to the times of our brothers.

What truths shall we remember of this time?
The truths of poverty, greed and avarice.
Yet are they not simply but grown up
and dressed as the philosophies of our time.

The Advert meets Reality

I went to a pub the other day
not one I much frequent.
But there it was in the advert
and it sort of looked OK.

Normally of course
I wouldn't dream of going
to such a dreadful dive.
Because,
I **have** been there before.

Still
its always sort of fun
to know reality.
A bit of reorientation
so to speak.

Yes, its really not like that
in real life.
Its more sort of crowded
smoky, unpleasant, with
dull people and loud DJ's.

Which is kind of funny really
as outside, somewhere else
the advert continues
to perpetrate its myth
on the unsuspecting.

Lines of verse

Line of
     verse
Followed by
     Line of verse
   Scratched on   paper
     First

by

this

pen

     Then by laser
     spraying
     effects on paper
     Echoing
     in
     the
     mind
                    Resonating
     images
     in
     the
     mind

Forms of   _____ communication

A series of

     Lines   _____
               _____
               _____
               _____
               _____
               _____
     of verse

Thanks for a wee New Year message

Why do I always fall for that old trick?
This ever encouraging view of romance.
A hand,
extended into private space.
Beckoning,
out to a dream beyond.
An image,
an ideal,
constant longing.

How and why should resistance build?
Searching (for) every new first brick.
The only chance to avoid the wall
rising to block the extended hand.
Leaving only solitary single thoughts.
So I always fall for that old trick.

Dark Star

Thursday July 11 1991
the darkening of the sun
engulfs Hawaii's islands.
The black sun appearing
from a bright summer day.
A footprint on July 11 1991.

A peculiarity of celestial geometry
unique to our third planet
displays the corona in all its glory.
The dark star displays its photosphere
in four minutes sixteen seconds
        of absolute totality.
The chromosphere also comes to light
driving the solar wind from Sol.

First contact eats the edge
as the moon marches across the face.
The sharpest crescent recedes to a sliver.
Hydrogen in the chromosphere glows spectral red.
A huge prominence hangs above the surface.

First light returns through the diamond ring
lighting the deepest valleys on the moons face.
The corona disappears and light emerges.

Poem for polling day, 1992

There are emerging signs
of disaffection
with this staged election.

Nothing has changed
Nothing has changed
Nothing has changed

Not a poll
Not a politician
Not a policy

No-one is taking any notice
of the disenfranchised voices
of the homeless, the poor,
of the sick, the hungry,
of the Scots.

This is the society we have now.
Must this be our fate.
Let's hope it's not too late,
and we have not forgotten how,
to change it now.

from a frontline living room

Last war poet

The last war poet has yet to come.
No sign on this horizon
of the last of our kind.

Still fiction to come of the deaths of our soldiers
dying in battles with armies like ours.

Why do they fight each other?
Preferably on neutral ground
always a cause,
wanting to be free.
This time to control the oil.

Next time, what will it be?

Take this question from me.
My use for it
is done.
No further purpose must it
serve.

Why Soldier?

What do you wish of me, soldier?
I have no time for war.
No argument with your mortal foe
must I concede is right.

What conflict calls you, soldier,
that I am compelled to follow?
And participate in bringing death
to those, you called fellows.

What noble cause of yours, soldier,
requires I take a life?
This championing of beliefs
requiring bullets and death.

What tribe needs me, soldier,
an outsider with words?
No stranger shall I kill
for a price, a shilling!

What need within you, soldier,
is greater than life itself?
No desire that I crave
this lust for glory.

What passion feeds you, soldier,
that cannot be refused?
This dinner, this diet of death,
to vile for normal bile.

Cont.

35

Cont.

What delights see you, soldier,
in the country that is future?
Where your every craft of death
is an abhorrence from the past.

What part of I are you, soldier,
hidden within us all?
So few who can refuse when called,
so few, so few.

Victoria's Cross

Come war, the simplest cross
calls farmers from toil.
Called for valour,
and spilling blood on foreign soil.

Come war, the simplest cross
alters in meaning
and men must die again,
falling for valour on foreign soil.

Another Saddam war

Once more we stand on the brink
Of war in a hot, distant land
Where the economics of oil drag us
To protect these black desert fields
Where a million men fresh from trenches
Defend the will of a new Saladin
Who defiles the new found child of peace
With his dreams of empire and glory
In a world readjusting to friendship
And nations return armies home quietly
The soldiers no longer required now
Yet one is still driven to soldier
And we must make ready, for war in Islam.

Medical call up November 1990

The preparations for war, go on as before
A wearisome task, even viewed from afar
Propaganda, powerful, persistent. persuasive

The preparations for war, come closer to home
More medics are called, as killing needs care
Personal, conscripted to care

The preparations for war, affect us all
Sleepwalking to war, blindfolded to peace
Passing rotation limits, talked out negotiations

The preparations for war, unstoppable now
Defeating crisis fatigue in fragile alliance
Resolutions, reinforcements, recruitment, resolve

The preparations for war, unavoidable now
Christmas parcels sent, the war comes after
C^3I in place, counting in days, dates and deadlines

The preparations for war, almost complete
Carols fill the Eastern desert, washing faces in winters fear
PONTI's ordered to the rear

The preparations for war, divide us all.

First tears fall

Preparing to count bodies again:
their number secret;
more blinded by mustard
on gas chamber duty.

Gruinard returning,
Brook Island re-trial.
Borrowed time approaches
on wars headlong agenda.

If I cannot be with you
at the beginning of this war
I shed my first tears on this page
Alone.

Day 4

I saw my first death today
Red flash, (on) Tornado, head-up display.
Obscuring information deluge,
blamed by most as refuge.

War in the air, on land and at sea.
Real oil, the only bleeding to see.

Visible to the world,
the first dead appear, Day 6, Tuesday.
The smoke-screen starts in Kuwait,
the truth will have to wait.

Genetic payment

What form of evolution
Brings this result of war
In the birthing of excess
Numbers of males

A strange balancing force
Exerted on us by nature
Programmed in our genes
Redressing the balance
Of mans despoiling folly

Last war correspondent

It is the final corner of the world,
which is only what you would expect.
This is not a simple tribal squabble
but a ten year long bloody civil war,
a war within a nation, bleeding the country dry.

Another year, another country, another war,
after the war to end all wars has been.
Before my time but a part of previous lives
in a reporting of the struggle for freedom,
fought by everyone, throughout their lives.

Can this be the last time of our lives
to fight our battles with the use of a gun?
Pursuing freedom by shooting our brothers,
creating divisions, families, peoples, races, nations,
to an end that has God and truth on its side.

Can this really, surely and certainly be
the last war to desecrate this world.
Can permanent peace be a dream of the past?
My work, does not yet seem completed,
for the world still feels, to wait for the next.

on the move

'Amazed Man' © Jim Dalziel

Poem of passage

Poems of passage
Written away from the lair
As moments snatched
From waiting or resting

Written away from the security
As incidents stolen
Seen or conjectured

Written adrift from the ties
As momentary notions
Hoping to gently hold

Written apart from the stream
As isolated dreams
Images of continuum

Written stops of reality
As visions snatched
Safely saved

Written atlas of the journey
As collected images
Poems of passage

Meeting a doubt ?

On my way to Tuvalu
I met an enquiring man.
He asked about you,
said he was you're biggest fan.

Its a long trip there,
so we had naturally got to talking.
He had a certain vocal flare,
a natural talent for storytelling.

We chatted about mutual friends,
both of us had known.
A means to ends,
as all other company had flown.

That was when he asked,
that slipped in question.
All about you subtly masked,
as simple friendship, without pretension.

My first reply was genial, bland,
'doing well', and making a joke.
Not intending sleight of hand,
he seemed to be a decent bloke.

And similarly on we went,
a pleasing way to pass a journey.
Each pursuing our natural bent,
to conversation as opening play.

Cont.

Cont.

Then came the second thrust,
with a marked, more probing feel.
And a sense of danger felt,
of unease, a shiver of steel.

Naturally, my reply gently parried,
curious of his knowledge and intent.
But in response, he only dallied,
making light, with an easy jest.

And similarly on we went,
a pleasing way to pass a journey.
Each pursuing our natural bent,
for conversation as closing play.

We arrived at Tuvalu,
parting without leaving a clue.
What secret did he know of you,
leaving a taste of something blue;
hinting of something only he knew.

Bayeux Tapestry Threads

What wonder to see a thousand years hence.
Looking back to a seemingly simpler time
of knights, gallant, upright and moral.
And changeless fiction on a painted backcloth.

A show of art and strength presented
in a dim and solemn technological cave.
While infra-red whispering academic voices
detail panels artistic as pages of history.

A story set to beguile, in brilliant threads.
Embroidered to shape panels as pictures
of momentous events and divided loyalties.
Portrayed one-sided as a visual cloth.

Reflections of Mantova

Confined by shore, a finger pointing
past waters edge, a burnt hazy horizon.
Graceful town, three lakes, four squares
with cornered bridges, extending where?

Interlocking squares, grand castled piazzas
internal chess with an eastern hue.
The blood of our saviour, sacred held
for a strange, somewhat short, thousand years!

Quietly waiting, empty for an occasion,
all present there, black and white squares.
Erupting sound, when celebrating here.
Closed town, to outsiders here.

Rouen

Trimming the trees
Of springtime's early buds
Leaving lifeless limbs
And cold naked wood

Rouen's regimented rows
An affront to nature
Sculpted so surreal
To leave nothing to reveal

Days of looking backwards and forwards

Just seem to follow us around
as a slowly accumulating set.
Packing them up from a long way out
marked 'wanted on voyage'.

Every chance encounter leads us here.
To think it is to make it so.

On the quayside, Saint-Nazaire, France

Sur le TGV

Marseilles Paris, lightning time, entrain.
Reservations issued, accepted cost, valueless paper.
Overbooking travellers, is standard issue.
Best seat obtained, with companion retained.
Avignon, Valence, briefly threaten standing.

Now direct, secure, speed beckons on.
How fast, what peaks of speed ahead.
Creeping, naturally, restricting Lyon interrupts.
Bizarrely passed by cars on train.

Acceleration, quickening, excitement more
humming speed, mixing rushing air.

Smooth and level on hissing track.
Percussion shock, signals crossing path.
Still gaining, illegible trackside signs.
Impressions blur and stomach tightens.
Odd squeak and noises needing oiling,
as outside crawls receding backwards.
Downhill stages are plunging headlong,
nerves concerned with stopping time and distance.

Yet smooth again, a vision of green.
Repeat percussion's seem less fierce
as rural idylls compare the centuries.

Walking forward, bouncing, jostling,
to compressed air services, pedal delivered.
And standing drinking, rocking and rolling,
to consider driving, a land based rocket.

Cont.

Cont.

Vitesse accepted, expected normal,
percussion's only passage time.
Till distant passing orange blur reminds,
relentless, pressing, velocity forward.

Percussion's stay frequent, edgy reassurance,
lessening now, with passings quiet.
Paris and slowing, both approaching.
Trackside view prolonged, considered, without haste.
Contrawise passengers now visible to view.
Scraping and tilting, final constricting corners.
Timely arrival, Gare de Lyon.

Palma Main Square

Back in Palma main square
There is a definite certain flair
With bustling locals, bemapped tourists
Flocks of white doves fed by purists
The guardia civil menace traffic
Holstered handguns for macho chic

A square of ever ceaseless transit
Two bus stations easily command it
Two vintage railways side by side
Stream the tourists island wide
A hub as true as ever found
For people moving round and round

Continuous traffic circles and circles
A clash of taxi horns always jangles
Every few minutes another crash
The cars monotonously bash and smash
With a tranquil green centre here
Back in Palma main square

Mallorca is full

Everywhere is completo
tonight, this town, this island, is full
twenty, thirty, forty, fifty hotels
or more, all have said full.

I've walked the tourist seafront
the place is fit to bursting
this El Arenal new Blackpool
not a single hotel space for hire.

It started badly in Puerto Soller
ten hotels full, bad premonition there
then the fiasco at El Arenal
already homeward urge grew fair.

So back to Palma, a city for sure
hotels a plenty, rooms everywhere
but the first half dozen or so on foot
defeated all optimism of sleep.

Inner turmoil growing strong
fight like fury and get a taxi
search in style and with flair.
Ask for help from locals here.

The map suggests a likely place.
Close to others at walking pace
perhaps expected it is not there
this is not exactly flair.

More of the same with growing despair.
Another ten completos everywhere, then

Cont.

Cont.

another taxi, a fellow traveller at this fair
already searched more, twice as far!

Ten more confirms the story
exactly what I need not bore you.
Its time to give up surely
and head to the airport, somewhat poorly.

The driver guide becomes appalled,
more he knows, though some are rich.
And yet six more, bring no surprises
let realists concede, out to the airport.

En route a final change of heart
realism over, lets try on the way
the local village may offer a chance.
Yet here again the story is the same.

So take me to the airport
I concede defeat in staying here.
Time to leave, I have been fair
no stone unturned, I have been thorough.

And now Miss Representative
surly though you may be.
Seen it all before I'm sure
all I ask is a simple standby.

Sit in the bar and wait I'm told
no sooner ordered than begun.
I'll standby drinking canias from now on
perhaps you'd better not make it too long.

on postcard landscapes

'Beached Writer' © Jim Dalziel

Italian Birds

Lots of delicate, small, Italian birds
in multicoloured hues, nay plumage too.
Artistically, even poetically arranged,
on a dinner plate for two.

Doors no More

Mondays, Firenze, surprisingly,
paradise is open to view.
The doors deported, dismantled,
arranged, encased and squared.
Ghiberti's Portal: Lost and Closed.

Haiku Two for You

News through the air
blown across the land.

News arriving, coming by air
single visitor, about to land.

Requiem for Athina

Trees of wind blend cicadas
to sunset sound
of sharp spirit and salt sea.

Sunset afire west Athina horizon
burning the air away.
To weep the grease of death
over darkening city streets.

What DH Lawrence thinks about Tourists

"There's nothing left to see anymore,
 everything's been looked at to death."

Fortunately you don't believe that
(and are still looking).
So you've read
these few lines

and remain
only a tourist.

from a possible future

Hubble telescope 'Ultra Deep Field'
1,000,000 seconds recording showing 13 billion years

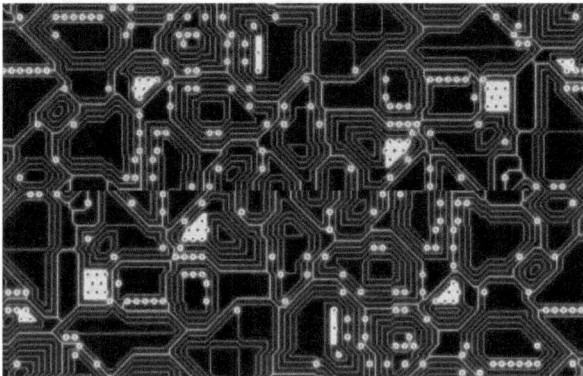

Cyberdream

Moving through space
in singularity cyberdream
computer generated
virtual reality
from software algorithms
running real-time
simulation simulacra
interfaced neuraly
by parallel port
to sleepless mainframes
of remote hosts
seeking artificial
intelligence.

This program will reach Jupiter in 22 minutes.

Virtuality

Escaping into cyberspace.
Through the window of virtual reality.
A light second from the stereopticon.

Existence within data
part of the information space .
Addict of the extra dimension
where we are knowledge.
Escaped from the real world
　　　　Into the datasphere.

Next Generation

Virtual reality fear
New living environment
Interfaced with silicon
Evolving alien life

Early organic chemistry
Predicting theoretical existence
Cousin to carbon
Beside us on Sol

Partnership awaiting Germanium
Darwin missed this
Infant to the man
Homo Siliconis

The Net

The net hides behind mirrorshades
reflecting world vision via silicon chips.
Multiple parallel linkages and interfaces
spread to encircle a hungering race.

Processing constantly, input data
into packaged bits for light delivery.
Bytes arriving for electronic storage
in machine readable binary code.

Information as data, now encrypted
in assembly language accessible to whom.
Expert systems written to judge this?
Then judge us?

Body Bank

Harvesting our bodies
for deaths spare parts.
Bits of possibility
to transplant to others
in need of deaths life.

No longer mortal

No longer mortal
after the end point is banished
and an eon of time
stretches ahead as vacant space.
The plaything of a liberated
burgeoning demanding human race.

No longer mortal
after the advent of times elixir
locking DNA in perpetuity.
But the loss of replication
ends the creativity
of time's addicts, consumers only now.

No longer mortal
after the loss of deaths virginity
kills the future forever.
Deconstructing the inner soul
leaving naked trembling psyches
as no longer mortal man shivers.

at last

Immortality the easy way

I will describe a miracle,
to be performed after my death.
Then will you consider me saint.

This miracle I will describe is -
the reading of this poem.
Sorry, not much of a saint.

'A sudden gust of wind at Ejiri' Hokusai

a quantum figure entangled

a figure entangled

a figure

吉米·因够斯医生

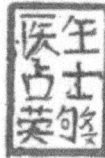

fractals & mnemonics

jamie inglis

fractals & mnemonics

Jamie Inglis

Contents

cont.

Contents cont.

from France

'Breton Band' © Jim Dalziel

Early light in Saint-Remy

Heats the mornings air for boules
beyond the clean wood
where metal jars the silent air.
Single sharp pastis starting
springs first mistless day.

Unchilling the pavement seats.
Where sharp short blacks
awake afresh the sense
of living here, Saint-Remy, today.

Flamingo Fire

At darkening time
on Lyon landscape
the flamingos fire
the fading sky.

Wheels of flame
spiral high overhead
riding the thermals
rising from the Camargue.

Waiting in Soulliac

One hundred tables
laid every day.
One hundred tablecloths,
covers, cutlery, glasses, plates, dressing,
correct each way.
Two hundred settings,
laid for those who will pay.

One hundred tables,
cleared every day.
Two hundred dishes,
for tourists who didn't stay.
One weary waiter,
at the end of every day.

Cyrano in Bergerac

A poet fresh, from a play
set in concrete, here to stay.

Just a bit, of a liberty
considering he never
passed this way.

Bergerac, France May 1992

Choosing a Tattoo on the Train to Bergerac

What best suits you
from the catalogue in view.
As the train rattles through,
which one to pursue.

The strangers are gaping
as they see you in the making.
A multitude of signals,
yours for the taking.

Something small and simple
to hide that hated pimple,
or complement that dimple.
Perhaps a rose, on a pink nipple.

A Gothic patch to cover your back
but don't want to look like a motorcycle hack.
You're name, of course, for when I get back.
Where to place, that's the right track.

Bordeaux Gare

Above Bordeaux gare
a single drapeau gently flaps
as darkness lightly drops.
And balls of light flicker bright
an orange glow of spheres alight
illuminate the station bright.

Buses halt, disgorge, depart.
Traffic becomes taxis then goes.
Information signs flickering without ceasing.
Late cafes catch the last stragglers.
The jazz notes drift on the square.
A bright gare clock strikes the end of day.

from Albania

Durres Beach, Albania, 1993

For Mijellin

When I listen, all I hear
are the songs of the heart, of poverty and sadness.
And when I look, all I see
are signs of the mind, painful to see.

What do I know of this world here
so distant from mine.
My life feels so out of time
that I must retreat to my dream.

Why, when I ask, is this so strange
the answers come tumbling but senseless.
For here this is real, if only tonight,
and tomorrow, we shall all wake to this.

Tirana Medicine

He showed me his container.
It was for the ulcer drug,
Ranitidine.
And it was empty.

I recognised the drug.
Very expensive,
my boss is on it,
(he's under a lot of stress you know),
swears by it.
Can go out, have a few drinks,
feel fine.
Not in Tirana,
with his empty container.

Memorial to the Martyrs, Durres, Albania 1993

Martyrs of 39

The memorial to the martyrs of 39
has faded now, and the glass is all gone.
Pillboxes fill the tranquil gardens,
where old men sit, playing chess
and reminiscing of these bright days.
Before the photos were removed,
and the martyrs became faceless.
Now their glory and their grace is gone,
the garden to weeds and war preparations.
Their fight is a long time over,
and the next already begun.
These brave martyrs, soon dust and gone.

Tirana, Albania 1993

Skandeberg Square, Tirana 1993

Early evening coffee at the Palace of Culture

The heart of Skandeberg
sings in the darkness.
A thousand voices ache
in poverty and sadness.

After the heat of the day
every space is part of the crowd.
Making a little, little business,
not a single head is bowed.

Islam wails from the new minaret
opposite communist murals, proclaiming Albania.
The old ideas are hard to forget
as market fever grips Tirana.

In the heart of Skandeberg
the deals are constantly done.
But poverty and sadness, are constant things,
no future will be harder won.

Durres Promenade

When I miss you most
is when the sun is sinking into the sea.
And the last rays cast a chill glare
along the seafront of people walking.
Mostly they are couples courting or together.
Sometimes with young babies
or sometimes with children in Sunday best.
Then there are the girls, also dressed
holding hands, in two's and three's.
And the young men their macho best
all walking in the twilight promenade.
And I sit as they pass and stare.
This is when I miss you most.

Nature whispers the loudest song

Drinking raki in the rain
under a flickering Durres lighthouse beam.
While the storm rages up the Adriatic
sheets of lightning curtain the horizon.
Thunder rocks the ice in the glass
as the coffee chills in the raindrop deluge.

Then, as the storm moves on past,
and while the glow from the raki still lasts;
a dazzling flash horizon long;
and thunder booming, on and on;
reminding us,
nature whispers the loudest song.

Enver Hoxha Museum, Tirana, 1993 (now Pyramid of Tirana)

Tirana

Different Eyes

So many landings
in different times
in different places.

So many landings
as different people
among different friends.

So many landings
from different lives
for different reasons.

So many landings
to different views
and different eyes.

from a frontline living room

Unloading at Prestwick

I see a coffin on TV today.
A homecoming coffin,
a local coffin, coming home.
Crying at death,
no longer faceless.
Now a face,
removed by fire of war.
Only the rictus remains,
and the lack of understanding.

Wikipedia Commons

Gulf War One plus one

One year passes from the start of war
hidden it continues obscured from view.
Many peoples forgotten after the storm
destroyed our homes, poisoned our land.

Alone in the mountains far from shelter
the touch of cold, twist of hunger.
Slowing each body, starving each mind
destroying our lives, driven from our land.

Alone in the desert far from shelter
poisoned black oases and darkness descending.
Expelled waste, herded and evicted
destroyed our people, lamenting our land.

Final letter

After he came home, sealed from view,
a day had passed, perhaps two.
When pain came
unbidden again.

A letter from the shadows
before death, out of time flows.
A final, final parting word
no way to send back a reply.

from Cyberville

'*Boffin*' © Jim Dalziel

Mockquake

Every year
when they practice
the Mockquake in Tokyo
it rocks the world.

The six wise men
of seismological science
announce abnormal data.
So take to the land.

The pulse to the city
starts out to sea
and takes nine seconds
to reach the superstructures.

Where tremors fracture
gas, glass and bodies.
Silence from Tokyo
shakes the world.

New Words For Today

Confidential

In Confidence

Draft in Confidence

In Strict Confidence

Commercial in Confidence

Restricted Access

Most Secret

Password protected

Patent Pending

Virus Checking

Unauthorised Possession is Illegal

Secret Society

Publication Prohibited

Ode to Postscript Printers

We thought we were clever

when we invented computers.

But they got viruses too.

New ones every day,

infected like us.

And passing it on

and on, and on, and on,

ανδ ον, ☺■ ♫🗁 □■ □□□□□□,

Error Message :   Programme has crashed

Error Message :   Programme has crashed

Error Message :   Programme has crashed

C:\>System access failure #13

General Protection Fault0M075P038

Switch off and call your helpline

Burgerland

Back in Burgerland
where no-one cares
what they eat or shit.

McDonalds promise to brighten up our lives
as the forests vanish
warming the planet degree by degree.
Then it seems our lives will brighten
as the sun heats our sky.

Back in Burgerland,
cardboard in,
cardboard and greenhouse gasses out.
Convenience is King.

i'm not loving it campaign

Pinball Graveyard

Where do all the old machines go?
When the electromagnets weaken,
the flippers begin to stick,
and the silver ball looses its shine.

Where do all the old machines go?
When the lights fail to flash,
the bumpers fail to bounce,
and the tilt is no longer a tremble.

Where do all the old machines go?
When the specials always light,
the excitement begins to fade,
and everyone scores the replay.

The New Alchemists

Smart machines modelling nature
Smart structures from the
New alchemists
Smart models

Smart molecules
Smart materials

Smart textiles
Smart piezo-electrics
Smart satellites
Smart buildings
Smart new alchemist

Soft ? brains

AI Thinker *RFID* Tool

eventually

Black hole passing a star (NASA/JPL)

Earth's time of darkness comes again

Late start,
to the fluorocarbon debate.
The herald of oblivion,
to the time of darkness again.

Depletion of the ozone layer,
means hide from the sun.
Three thousand years ago
Bronze age Scotland
changed forever.
This change forever comes again.

It was once a very different world
when a generation of Scots
will once again abandon their land,
leaving the wasteland,
far to the north.

The dusting of Hecla III
went unnoticed in 1150,
but the trees stopped growing.

Cont.

cont.

Volcanos, acid, poor climate,
slows the trees.
Marasmus, Rabal, Etna, Santorini, Krakatoa, Tambura.

The time of darkness,
comes again.
Benjamin Franklin's first conjecture,
leads to Tambura,
and the year without a summer, 1816.
During the obscuration of the sun,
Byron speaks Darkness.

The aerosols spread round the stratosphere,
scattering the sunlight,
chilling the oceans.
Winters chilling.

The ozone deviation has appeared.
Chlorofluorocarbons sensitised the trigger
for the next big volcano to erupt.

Hearts of Darkness

Hearts of darkness
pacing empty city streets.

Isolated and alone, fleeing
the fray of life in the city,
whose heart has gone.
Bled away, by greed and fear,
by hearts so blue.

How could they do this thing
to hearts that were young.
Before they became
hearts of darkness.

The end of The Lakes

The lakes are shrinking and dying
    shrivelling, as new land appears around their rims.

The lakes are poisoned, gasping and dying,
    polluted waters soak the land.

Lake Baikal, the great lake is dying,
    the steppes spreading, shrinking the shore.

Lake Chad, the desert lake is dying,
    the Sahara spreading further south.

The largest lakes are dying first,
    as the earth begins, a nightmare thirst.

Empty Cardboard Box

I do not waste my dreams on sleep
I dream my dreams by day.

Living these dreams
I am just unable to lock away.

I do not dream of islands
but follow the flow by day.

Living these dreams
in the harsh light of play.

I do not dream of flying
nothing clouds my dreams by day.

Living this dream
of finding somewhere to stay.

more new neologisms

www.newneologisms.com

104

InfoBlur

Adrift amid oceans of expanding information,
at our fingertips and before our eyes.

Six billion data trails and all human knowledge,
at our fingertips and before our eyes.

www.infoblur.com

GiGaDust

A supervolcano shakes the planet's plates,
the ejecta slowly darkens the sun.

Massive dust clouds merge around the planet,
gigadust forms and leads to winter.

www.gigadust.com

TimeTAPS

Shocks from the cracks in history,
events out with the human record.

Outliers from the land of the past,
change out with the human record.

www.timetaps.com

ChaoDays

Emerging strings of chaotic events,
merge and menace normal time.

Butterfly signs each and every day,
buffet and bruise normal time.

www.chaodays.com

LogoBLUR

Corporate icons fade to grey.
Corporate mantras forgotten today.

Corporate religions lose their way.
Corporate empire has had its day.

www.logoblur.com

TimeExit

Step outside the constant flow,
freeze each moment before the next.

An Einstein bridge outside time,
living each moment before the next.

www.timeexit.com

colophon

Some friends
from afar
visit today
and somehow
seem, to stay,
even after
they, have gone.

'A sudden gust of wind at Ejiri'   Hokusai

吉米·因够斯医生

112

hold on

jamie inglis

hold on

JAMIE INGLIS

Contents

Cont.

Cont.

Operation Market-Garden

There are some places you visit
where the ghosts are very vocal

Operation Market-Garden

Operation Market-Garden
the idea was unstoppable.
Again that old military lie
'We'll all be home for Christmas'.

Main route into Arnhem

Landing at DZ-X

Landing at DZ-X
that quiet Sunday afternoon
of September seventeen.
Time enough to make char.

Only ten sticks of men on the lion route
will reach the north end of John Frostburg.
This day.

Across the fields to the bridge

Original bridge rebuilt in 1948. Renamed John Frostburg in 1977

Walking the Lion Route

Walking the lion route in the pouring rain.
Down from the airborne cemetery into Oosterbeek
two field hospitals stand exposed at the crossroads.
Back to headquarters at the Hartenstein
the airborne memorial a spike in the gloom.
Down to church that will be the escape
and set out on the lion route, the low road to town.
First the railway bridge blown in our faces.
Then Nelson Mandelaburg new to the town
a quiet shelter from the torrential rain.
Halfway to the bridge, stop at the promenade.
On in the rain, a downpour to believe.
A final rest under the ramparts.
Then the stairs up to the ramp
and a moment or two standing in silence.
Here to remember
and for a moment the sun shines.

Here to remember

I am of the next generation
to follow after these brave men.
It is our deathly obligation
to visit after these brave men
and follow their steps until they fell.
To listen to the stories of these brave men
telling of their comrades never going home.
To remember here these brave men
and see again their bloody, needless, end.

The Airborne Cemetery

The airborne cemetery,
the only one in the world.
For men with wings
who dropped from the sky
over Arnhem that fateful day.

An airborne cemetery,
for those seventeen hundred men.
Who will forever rest here
in a field near Oosterbeek
after dropping in battle in the days to come.

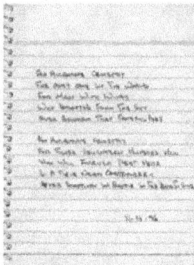

11.11.96

124

Armistice Day 11.11.96

Another cemetery for tears

Another cemetery for tears
far too many over the years.
What happened, to all our fears?

Another cemetery for tears
more soldiers forever held dear.
Resting in a field forever near.

Another cemetery for tears
white military headstones and neat rows here.
Always the price is way too dear.

some earlier

One hand speaking

Speaking with one hand
The scratch of pen on paper
Speaking through the air
To those who will listen

Speaking with one hand
Attempting to scratch the pain
Of speaking to you out there
Hoping that someone will listen

Speaking with one hand
Scratching down another page
Nearly finished speaking now
Is anyone still listening?

Finding a church at home

As soon as I walked through the door
I knew it was a religious service,
such things are ever the same.
Recognisable in every life
as a hushed contemplative awe
in silent cloistered worship sites.

And when the door crashed closed behind me
and I twisted to confront this traitorous noise
and twisted back to the eyes of the congregation
and stood as close as I could to a faint
and then waited for the service to end.

The Matter Gap
(No More Big Bang)

Late piece of the jigsaw doesn't fit
Last few pieces forced into the wrong hole
This is the end of the beginning
Started 15,000 million years ago
At 10^{-35} seconds
Storm in a cosmological tea cup
The galaxies showed red shift and
were deemed to be expanding and departing
by Hubble in 1939

Penzius and Wilson heard the radio echo
of that first bang in 1965

More than enough to keep on expanding
We are at the critical mass density
Ten times more matter than we have found
Where is all this cold dark matter

Then come the stick men and galactic holes
Large scale structures of clustered galaxies

Too many large structures
For cold dark matter prediction
So no more Big Bang

Voting with their feet
(the refugees of circumstances)

The exodus of the century closes the millennium.
Everywhere, refugees mass in great numbers
crushing against the borders of state and mind.
Pressing the boundaries, desperate,
numbing pain and belief, contorting the truth,
of a shimmering safety mirage, uselessly apparent
at the end of a conviction that help is near.

Only the refugees of precarious circumstances,
forced to depart the peril of a nation's situation
disturbing the ability to stay and survive.
This tortuous displacement of surviving life.
Voting with their feet,
the refugees of circumstances.

Bloody Balkans

Small States Again

Returning to the time of small states.
When there was Thrace
at war with Macedonia.
And the world was tribes again
disputing over ground,
that was rightfully theirs,
since the time of there forebears.

And the small state comes again.
Our civilisation is ending,
as so many others have before this,
by descending into anarchy.
Small states again.

Defending our chickens

Getting worse in Sarajevo town
as the convoys stop
and night falls.

Shells in the night
gunfire in the night
tracers in the air.

Illuminating our huddles
lit by candlelight
and never silent.

Sarajevo the siege.
When will it end?

Goradze

A wounded city
out in the open.
Obliterated from view
by poor communication.

The observer has retired
only the volunteers remain.
Easing the cities pain
from birth to oblivion.

World War CCC

World War III
has not turned out to be
the great conflagration
we expected it to be.

World War III
turned out to be
World War CCC.

Macedonia is a country again

Its official
Macedonia is a country again,
and to prove it
they've just beaten Liechtenstein 11-1.

The crowd will be going wild in the streets
of ehm, eh, ehm ......
Back to you in the studio Des.

PS 2019
North Macedonia is also a country.

Yesterday, Today and Tomorrow

Isosceles © Jim Dalziel

Barings goes down

The Barings butterfly.
A butterfly in far off Singapore.

A butterfly flaps his wings
in far off Singapore.
Flaps his wings
and the oldest bank is no more.

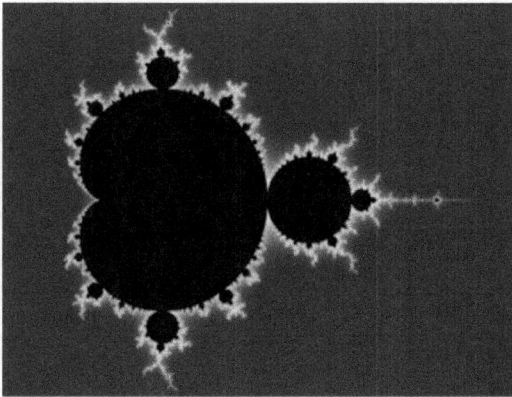

Chaos theory in action

For Bao Ninh

Amidst the sorrow of war
I will see you here.

Wait for me here
after you have waited forever.

Amidst the sorrow of war
waiting will hurt no more.

Wait for me here
make me be here.

Wreath Street, Hanoi 1994

Amsterdam coffee shop

Watching over the children, who sit
aimlessly in small groups waiting.
Then the serious dealers appear waiting also.
The children keep rolling then the dealer
sits near and then so his friend.
They're rolling too but is it the same.
Let's see how they do this, this is their game.
No one is doing anything like thinking
everyone's playing their own game.
Sounds like it could be Morocco
who will play host to tonight's game.

That old refrain

Heading down to the clinic again
too many E's and speed again.

Heading down to be there again
another first night, wherever, again.

Heading down to the clinic again
expecting to hear much the same.

One more time with that old refrain
something perhaps, to ease the pain.

Maybe Einstein was wrong

What if Einstein was wrong
and we could travel faster than light (ftl).
A very early acronym for those collectors
of such interesting pieces of arcane linguistics.

Still, I digress,
what if Einstein was wrong.

Well,
how could it be done,
to fly us back in time.
Or should we just work on the assumption
that eventually some smart mathematician
will show us how it's done.
We are not mathematicians
so we assume one day it has been done.

Tattoo Times

Tattoos in our times
the jewellery of the poor
paid for permanency
an expression as a jewel.

an expression of love
an expression of power
an expression of nationality
an expression of ownership
an expression of slavery

Tattoos of our times
a jewelled expression of emotion
proudly visible
to inflame and ignite.

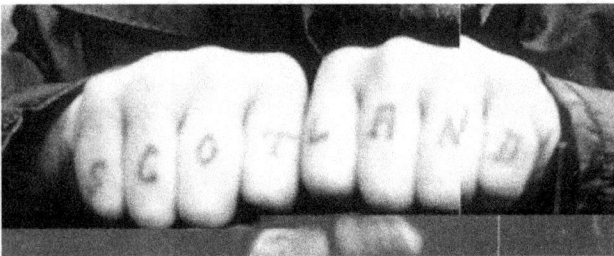

After the plague

After the plague
there were few of us left,
rattling around in the empty cities.
Wondering, what now?

Everyone had gone.
Everyone left was searching again
for friends,
to begin again.

Holding Patterns

people in holding patterns
they make me uneasy
as they wait for the clock
    to turn.

people in holding patterns
they make me wary
as they wait to decide
    what next.

A Good Netizen?

I spoke face to face
with a stranger, for the first time
half way round the world
they were there, and I was here.

Face to face by wire
over the web, winding us together.
Hi doc he said
I replied it was my first time.

Face to face in chat
What sort of doc? Where from?
Wow my dad's the same!
Thanks for the chat, got to go, bye.

Courier

Courier from culture to culture.
Courier of ideas to ideas.

The courier is the border
the courier is the mix
the courier is the new

sometimes flash
sometimes fame
sometimes forever

what courier to be
what courier to become.

A blank page to start
an idea to impart.
Don't listen, to that old *art.

more new neologisms

www.newneologisms.com

GiGaDark

Charged particles from the solar flare,
irradiate the infrastructure everywhere.

Charged particles from the solar flare,
lights out, lights out, everywhere.

www.gigadark.com

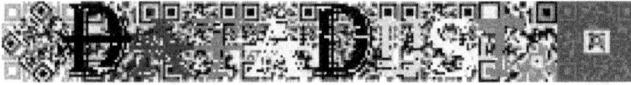

DataDust

Accumulating detritus of the information age,
binary code and pixels in our wake.

Debris left behind in the machine,
binary code and pixels are our wake.

www.datadust.com

ChaoList

Do not do this when that happens,
do this when that does not happen.

When this happens do not do this,
if this does not happen, do this.

www.chaolist.com

Chaologist

An expert or student of chaos,
however improbable that may be.

Predicting everything unlikely to you and me,
however improbable that may be.

www.chaologist.com

Anti-OrG

Where organisations fear to lead,
individuals change the world.

When organisations lead us astray,
you change the world.

www.anti-org.org

GiGaEcho

Some actions resonate beyond their limits,
returning changed in unimagined ways.

Every action ripples without limit,
spreading change in unanticipated ways.

www.gigaecho.com

colophon

This is my art

This is my art and this is me
what you get is what you see.
Don't ask me why this is me.

This is my art and this is me
what you see is what you get.
It's all of me and nothing yet.

'A sudden gust of wind at Ejiri' Hokusai

吉米·因够斯医生

next -

gluon notes

jamie inglis

Monument des Morts

Monument des Commandos

Armistice morning, Saint-Nazaire 11.11.00

At eleven 'o' clock
the old men wearing their medals
and the standard bearers and the band
gather with fanfare
at the monument des morts.

More medals are presented.
Brave speeches are made
to remember those who are dead.

The wreaths are laid.
The standards are lowered
and a hundred doves take to the air.

The band form up
and the old soldiers behind
march off with their memories.

One hundred yards down the quayside
the Monument des Commandos is quiet
no flags, no ceremony today.

Warriors of Xian

Acres of soldiers
arrayed in square fields
standing, made from clay.

Cavalrymen and horses
eerily silent
in the red earth.

A motionless army
still for centuries
waiting the millennia away.

A tomb of terracotta,
legions of patient warriors
waiting through eternity.

Warriors of Xian
guarding forever
The Emperor's future.

~~INFO~~Gale

A googolplex of information searched every day,
a blizzard of information received every day.

A knowledge hurricane coming this way,
page upon page of information blowing us away.

www.infogale.com

Jamie Inglis is a poet and doctor from Edinburgh.

His poems are about travelling near and far, of times, places
and who we are. Poems about the unexpected and the
unexplained and about wars fought in our name.
Poems of new words embedded in the web.

He has worked and published on a wide range
of public health issues including HIV, cancer,
immunisation, tobacco, drugs and obesity.

He had his first poems published aged ten and after
qualifying in medicine returned to writing poetry
in the early 1980's.

His poems reflect his interests in people, pacifism,
politics, travel, science–fiction, the world we live in
and the world we are creating.

After travelling round the world five times
he still lives in Edinburgh.

t g d
h e r
e o e
  m a
  e m
  t s
  e
  r
  s

jamie inglis

fractals & mnemonics

jamie inglis

hold on

jamie inglis

9 781916 354203 >

吉米·因够斯医生

© **Prohibited** Publications
MMXX
www.prohibitedpublications.com

www.ingramcontent.com/pod-product-compliance
Lightning Source LLC
LaVergne TN
LVHW051637080426
835511LV00016B/2366